The Manatee Scientists

Saving
Vulnerable
Species

By Peter Lourie

12/13/16
To Kathryn —
Keep Exploring

HOUGHTON MIFFLIN HARCOURT
Boston   New York

For Erica

Acknowledgments

I would like first and foremost to thank manatee scientists John Reynolds, Fernando Rosas, and Lucy Keith Diagne, who gave so much of their time and patience in the making of this book. What wonderful work they are doing to understand and protect the world's three vulnerable manatee species. Thanks to scientists Dana Wetzel, James "Buddy" Powell, Gordon Bauer, Benjamin Morales, Vera da Silva, and Robert Bonde, who made it possible for me to enter the world of the manatee. Thanks also to Sarita Kendall, who has been working on manatees in the Colombian Amazon for ten years and has helped eliminate hunting in that area. A special thanks to my buddy Steve Swinburne, a wonderful naturalist and fine writer (the author of *Saving Manatees*). I'd like also to thank "Captain Joe" Detrick who runs Fun 2 Dive, the best manatee swimming operation in Crystal River, Florida. What makes his business stand out is that he takes only small groups and insists that swimmers don't harass or touch or even approach manatees unless the manatees approach first. He instills both respect and awe for the creatures and for the laws that were established to conserve them. In an age when some manatee operations are literally throwing forty or fifty people into the water with these gentle giants, Joe still keeps his groups to six or fewer. Finally, a special thank-you to my wonderful editor at Houghton Mifflin, Erica Zappy, whose love for and fascination with manatees has been the driving spirit behind this book. Erica is as energetic as her name suggests. Her boundless love of books, science, and adventure motivates authors and readers to be their best selves.

For information about permission to reproduce selections from this book, write to trade.permissions@hmhco.com or to Permissions, Houghton Mifflin Harcourt Publishing Company, 3 Park Avenue, 19th Floor, New York, New York 10016.

www.hmhco.com

The text of this book is set in Latienne and Century Gothic.
The Library of Congress has cataloged the hardcover edition as follows:
Lourie, Peter.
The manatee scientist : saving vulnerable species / written by Peter Lourie.
p. cm. — (Scientists in the field) Includes bibliographical references and index.
1. Manatees—Conservation—Juvenile literature. 2. Marine mammalogists—Juvenile literature. I. Title.
QL737.S63L68 2011   599.55092'2—dc22   2010009739

ISBN: 978-0-547-15254-7 hardcover
ISBN: 978-0-544-22529-9 paperback

Manufactured in China
SCP 10 9 8 7 6 5 4 3 2 1
4500577858

Contents

A Florida manatee surfacing for air.

Prologue

In Crystal River, Florida, a ten-foot, twelve-hundred-pound manatee glides, then gently turns on its back to float upside down, its flippers tucked up against its chest, making it look like a rolling, playful dog. Its eye, quiet, gray, embedded in lined, elephant-like skin, inspects the mammal's surroundings as it rolls again and again. Manatees are like overgrown puppies.

Years ago, sailors somehow mistook manatees for mermaids, and as a result, manatees fall into a group of animals called sirenians. They are as uniquely captivating as the Sirens for whom they are named—the mythical sea nymphs from Homer's epic *The Odyssey* who sang bewitching songs, luring lovesick sailors to their island, where the sailors' ships smashed against the rocks. But these unlikely modern sirens enchant without peril.

Manatees are aquatic herbivores. They eat mostly plants and grasses. To support their large bodies, they eat for hours and hours every day. They have no natural enemies in some parts of their range. Yet even in Florida, where they are protected by law (you are not allowed to touch or approach a manatee unless it approaches you first), the species is endangered, at risk of becoming extinct. In fact, all three of the world's manatee species are extremely vulnerable to extinction.

The Florida manatee, a subspecies of the West Indian manatee, is among the best studied of all marine mammals in the world. Scientists easily observe Florida manatees in the clear waters of places like Crystal River. This is not the case with the two other species, which live in the vast, murky waters of coastal Africa and the myriad rivers of the Amazon basin.

Spotting an African or an Amazonian manatee in clouded water is most

Florida manatees swimming upside down (top) and skimming the surface of the water (above).

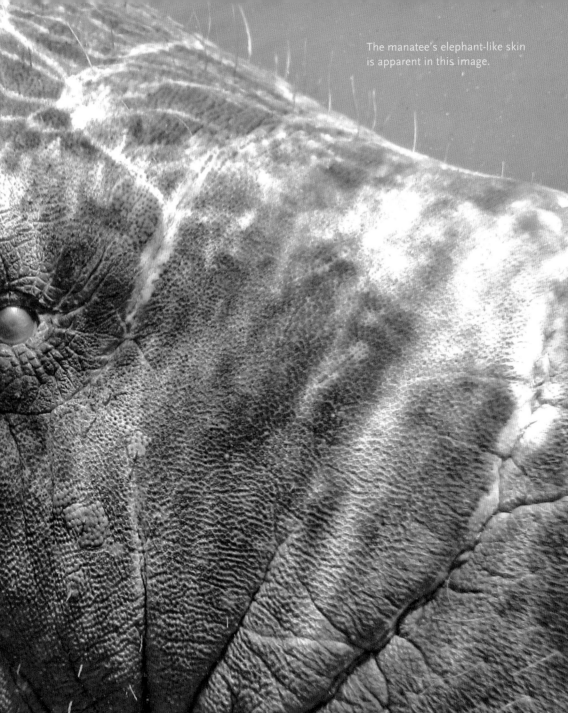

The manatee's elephant-like skin is apparent in this image.

Two Florida manatees swimming forward (above), and one rolling and turning, with its head down.

unusual. As a result of their "invisibility," as well as a lack of scientific studies in developing countries where food and money are scarce, these two other species are not as fully understood as the Florida manatee. If you're indeed lucky enough to spot an African or Amazonian manatee in the wild, it is usually just two nostrils on a river's surface or the ripple from a diving animal's fluke, or tail.

Since 1996, throughout the world, all three species have been included on the International Union for Conservation of Nature's (IUCN) Red List of Threatened Species as vulnerable or endangered. The gentle manatee is mainly threatened not by other animals but by humans—boats, industrial development and habitat destruction, accidental entanglements in nets, chemical contaminants (such as pesticides and petroleum, that may poison the animals), and deliberate hunting. In Africa and the Amazon, the manatee is still a food source, as it was in Florida in precolonial times. As recently as the late 1880s, people occasionally killed and ate manatees in Florida.

It isn't always simple to designate an animal as vulnerable or endangered, but it is a process that occurs in the hope of protecting the species. How do scientists establish an animal's level of endangerment, or what is called its conservation status? What scientific criteria are used to put any animal on the endangered list or take it off the list? What is the Red List and what do the categories on the list actually mean? More important, how

Two Amazonian manatees feeding on vegetation, with only their nostrils showing.

does a given designation help protect the animal?

When a species of plant or animal is given a designation on the Red List, it is put into a category such as extinct, critically endangered, endangered, vulnerable, near threatened, or not evaluated.

To arrive at these designations, researchers have developed and combined specific scientific methods. Some of these are as simple as counting animals and knowing where they are and how many of them exist, but according to manatee scientists in Sarasota, Florida, exciting new methods are just now being tested.

Even a moderate-size manatee takes a lot of hands and muscle to manage.

Exploring the world of the manatee to see how the species is faring often means jumping into a small plane, driving through a desert, or boating up a river. Three manatee scientists, each studying a different species, are doing just that, and there's no better way to understand the concept of conservation status than to join them on their adventures.

This Florida manatee floats in crystal-clear water.

IUCN Red List Categories

Species are classified in nine groups, determined by criteria such as rate of decline, population size, area of geographic distribution, and degree of population and distribution fragmentation. All three species of manatees fall into the vulnerable category, but this could change in the future as scientists learn more about them from traditional methods, such as assessing their population numbers, as well as from cutting-edge chemical and genetic analysis.

Extinct

Extinct (EX): No individuals remaining.

Extinct in the Wild (EW): Known only to survive in captivity or as a naturalized population outside its historic range.

Threatened

Critically Endangered (CR): Extremely high risk of extinction in the wild.

Endangered (EN): High risk of extinction in the wild.

Vulnerable (VU): High risk of endangerment in the wild. A vulnerable species is a species that is likely to become endangered unless the circumstances threatening its survival and reproduction improve. Manatees fall into this category.

At Lower Risk

Near Threatened (NT): Likely to become endangered in the near future.

Least Concern (LC): Lowest risk. Does not qualify for a more at-risk category.

Data Deficient (DD): Not enough data to make an assessment of its risk of extinction.

Not Evaluated (NE): Has not yet been evaluated against the criteria.

Amazon

Fernando talks with school kids in front of one of the manatee tanks at INPA in Manaus.

In the sprawling, overcrowded city of Manaus, Brazil, manatees are raised in captivity, where they can be closely studied. Manaus is one of the only places you can pet young Amazonian manatees, *Trichechus inunguis*. But before you pet them, you have to make a little noise in the water so they know someone is nearby. Then you can touch their silky-smooth skin when they put their snouts up for a baby bottle with milk in it.

"These manatees are our responsibility, and it's our fault if they die," says Dr. Fernando Rosas, a manatee scientist who is watching one of the workers feed a calf with a baby bottle. Fernando works at the Aquatic Mammals Lab at the National Institute for Amazonian Research (INPA) in Manaus. "To conserve Amazonian manatees and to establish their conservation status, the first thing we have to do is understand the animals. This is what we're doing here," he says. The manatee project began in 1974 with Dr. Robin Best, a Canadian manatee scientist, and one captive *peixe-boi* (pronounced "peh-shee boy"), which is Portuguese for manatee. The name means "ox, or bull fish." "But of course the manatee is not a fish. It is a mammal," Fernando says.

When Fernando first entered university, he decided to work with marine mammals because of a teacher who inspired him. He read about their biology, ecology, and conservation. "During my last year of university I wrote a proposal for a project about the use of manatees for controlling aquatic vegetation that grows in large quantities

Fernando feeding a young Amazonian manatee at the tank in Manaus.

Two Amazonian manatees swim in water dense with vegetation.

in hydroelectric lakes, huge reservoirs used for the generation of hydroelectric power. This vegetation causes a lot of problems. The plants are good places for mosquitoes to lay their eggs, and the vegetation eventually dies, and its decomposition increases the acidity of the water, which causes corrosion in the turbines and engines of the hydroelectric operations." Since manatees are herbivores that love to eat aquatic plants, Fernando had the idea to introduce manatees into the reservoirs in order to eat the vegetation and not to use poison to kill the plants. Little did he know at the time that Dr. Best in Manaus had had the same idea, and his project was already in progress when Fernando moved north to the Amazon.

In 1981 Fernando left southern Brazil for Manaus. "Well," he says, "Robin was very happy to see me, and in two days I was on a boat heading down the Amazon River to radiotrack manatees in a hydroelectric lake."

He tagged the manatees with a transmitter contained in a belt around the mammal's peduncle, the relatively narrow area between the body and the fluke. He then followed them with a radio receiver, keeping notes and studying their movements. From then until now, Fernando has always kept one foot (most of the time two feet) in the Amazon rainforest. He loves working in the jungle with manatees, as well as with giant otters and freshwater dolphins. "The experience of moving from southern Brazil to northern Brazil was a real adventure," he says. "I had to learn how to sleep in a hammock, since this is not

Two assistants measure a young manatee at INPA.

An assistant changes the water in a tank.

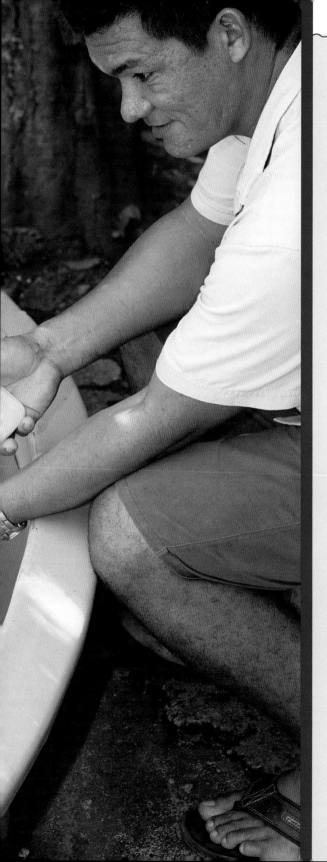

common in southern Brazil, and I must tell you that today I much prefer sleeping in a hammock than in a bed."

Fernando walks around the tanks outside his office, talking to the people who feed and care for the captive manatees. An adult manatee floats motionless in a nearby tank. Fernando says, "A lady called me the other day. She was hysterical because she saw a manatee floating and thought it was dead. No, I assured her, that's just what they do. They rest for long periods.

"Our baby manatees drinking milk from bottles—well, it touches your heart, but out there in the wild, most Amazonian people never see *peixe-boi*s. Even the hunters only see them when they catch them." Fernando admits that you'd get limited data if you depended only on wild Amazonian manatees. Having more than thirty captive animals in one place has been fantastic for long-term scientific studies.

It's helpful for researchers to have these captive manatees, but how did so many manatees get into the tanks? "Sometimes when hunting manatees,

A young manatee is fed with a baby bottle.

people on the river use the babies as bait to attract the mothers," he says. "They often don't know what to do with the babies when they're finished with them, so they bring the little ones to us here at INPA."

Studying captive animals has led to a better understanding of the Amazonian manatee's physiology—its physical and chemical functions and activities. Fernando says, "We have learned things such as how much they eat." He reads aloud some thesis titles of recent graduate students: "The Consumption Rate of Amazonian Manatees in Captivity," and "Transit Time of Food in the Digestive Tract of the Amazonian

An assistant interacts with a manatee in its tank.

Three young Amazonian manatees wait in their tank as it is refilled with fresh water.

ing to sex, or during pregnancy, for example. This information comes from our captive manatees." The first work on the metabolic rate of manatees in general was done in the Manaus lab in the late 1970s. "So why here?" he asks. "Because we have studies going on all the time. We have so many captive animals. In all of the U.S.A. there are maybe fifty captive manatees. But we have thirty-five in Manaus alone!"

Beginning in 1998, Fernando and his colleagues were able to breed manatees in captivity. "Now we have to try to reintroduce manatees into the wild, to increase the population of the species so they are no longer threatened." He smiles. "This is our challenge. And at the same time to embark on an extensive education program to get people to stop eating them."

Fernando hopes to release two more captive manatees into the wild again next year, even as they keep tabs on the two they released this year. The first Amazonian manatees ever to be released into the wild were two males, Puru and

Anama, thirteen and ten years old. Following them with a telemetric receiver that "hears" the small transmitter inside the belt fastened around their peduncles will, Fernando hopes, help him learn more about the movements of the manatees in the wild. All this new information will inform future releases of captive animals into the wild.

Today Fernando and one of his research assistants, Jeferson Barros de

Manatee in Captivity." This is the kind of information biologists can get only from studying manatees in tanks. "Yes, you can catch a manatee in the wild and collect some blood samples," Fernando says, "and you can take some basic information, then release the animal, but you can't follow the animal year after year, day by day. You can't learn how the blood changes according to age, accord-

A young girl with a pet chick along the Rio Cuieiras.

14

João Pena, a former manatee hunter, shows how he'd capture a manatee to eat.

Oliveira, will be going out to a tributary a few hours by boat from the big city in order to check on another research assistant, Diogo Alexandre de Souza, who, along with Jeferson, takes turns monitoring the invisible trails of Puru and Anama in the Rio Cuieiras. Fernando picked the Rio Cuieiras for release because there is little hunting of manatees in that area.

"We are thinking of releasing as many manatees as possible because our tanks are overcrowded. But it's not as easy as you might think. Fish reproduce thousands of times every year, but one female manatee has only one baby every three or four years." The "bull fish" does not reproduce like a fish at all. "The other problem," says Fernando, "is that our rivers are the supermarkets. People live on fish, and the taste of *peixe-boi* meat is completely different from their usual diet. People love it. They eat fish for breakfast, lunch, and dinner, so any change in this diet is welcome. This is why it is so difficult to stop people from killing the *peixe-boi*."

Amazonia is a big area—1.2 billion acres (or 5 million square kilometers) just in Brazil—so to change people's eating

A motor on a small canoe: a traditional engine used for shallow waters during the dry season.

habits will be very difficult. It's impossible for Fernando or the handful of other manatee scientists to go everywhere and tell people that manatees are so vulnerable. "Brazilian laws prevent people from killing a manatee for commercial purposes—a hunter is not legally allowed to sell its meat. But if he hunts a manatee for his own subsistence—and many people along the rivers are very poor and need what they can get from the river in order to survive—then it is legal."

Where the law gets fuzzy is when someone kills a manatee not to eat, but to sell the meat to buy staples for their family, like salt and sugar and rice. That person will say they are doing this to survive. And who can blame them?

Fernando and Jeferson grab their gear, hammocks, and some food for the two-day trip up the Rio Negro to Rio Cuieiras. In the port of Manaus they hop a small boat for the seven-hour journey.

Puru and Anama, when they were released, were placed in a floating mesh tank in the Cuieiras. They spent a week in the tank, submerged in the water to get accustomed to the river, then were let go. Fernando had known them for many years. Puru arrived at INPA in 1995; Anama had weighed only forty-four pounds when he first came to Fernando in 1998. Like the other captive manatees, these two had been bottle-fed for a year, then given vegetables and wild grasses. Before they were released, they underwent a battery of tests that checked their blood, urine, and respiration to make sure they were healthy enough to undergo the pressures of reintro-

A typical homestead on the Amazon.

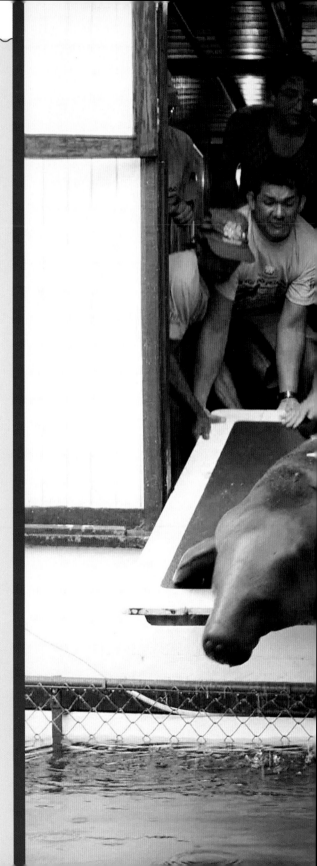

Release of Anama, one of the only two Amazonian manatees released into the wild.

A riverboat on the Amazon.

The INPA house used by Diogo and Jeferson while they track manatees.

duction into the wild, a place they'd never seen, a river that has many more dangers in store for the manatees than a tank in Manaus.

The water level of the Cuieiras drops fast as the dry season approaches. In some parts of the Amazon, this drop can measure up to forty-five feet. The Rio Cuieiras runs through what in Portuguese is called an *igapó,* or blackwater forest, a type of flooded Amazonian forest that has lower nutrients in its soil, lower biomass, and lower diversity than other flooded forests in the region. Fewer insects and fewer animals, too.

"We picked this kind of river for a number of reasons," says Fernando. INPA has a small hut in the area, which Jeferson and Diogo can use as a base for the days and months they are following the two manatees. Also there is a good relationship here between the scientists and the community, an important ingredient in many scientific endeavors. When scientists work in a community that is open to their work, it makes it much easier to enlist local help. "Most important, though," says Fernando, "there seems to be no recent hunting of manatees on the Cuieiras."

VHF radio transmitters inside belts were placed around the peduncles of the two animals so the scientists could follow them to learn more about their movements, their behavior, and their preferred habitat. After an initial time together, the two manatees separated, and they have remained separated ever

17

Chiqúinhó wades through water in the forest as the group searches.

Jeferson holds an antenna and points into the forest as Fernando follows him.

since. For the past five months, Jeferson and Diogo have taken turns hiring local river pilots to follow the two animals. Every day they go out with a local river pilot named Chiqúinhó and take GPS readings of the manatee travels. They also test the water's cloudiness, or turbidity, and depth, and they try to take samples of plants the manatees may be eating.

The assistants have reported that one of the manatees, Puru, has not moved in a month. Fernando fears that a hunter or a jaguar may have killed him. He hopes, however, that the radio belt has simply slipped off the animal's body. It could be lying somewhere in the shallows of this blackwater river. Fernando and the guys will try to find it.

Racing up a small tributary of the Cuieiras, Chiqúinhó skims the glassy black water as the banks of the river narrow; then he comes to a stop. Bird and insect noise punctuates the humid air. When Diogo pulls the receiver and the antenna out of a case and assembles

it, it starts to chirp every one or two seconds. The sound grows stronger when the antenna is pointed toward the location of the transmitter. This is Anama.

Someone sees a rippling on the water and says, "It's a manatee." Another says it's a *boto,* a river dolphin, but Chiqúinhó swears it's Anama himself. "Manatees are so timid," says Fernando. "We are very close; you can tell by the intensity of the sound of the receiver, but we can't see him. And we probably won't!"

Fernando doesn't use satellite tracking as they do in Florida. His transmitter system requires that he must be within .6 miles (1 kilometer) to get a signal. When either Jeferson or Diogo loses the animal, he travels up and down the river very slowly until he gets a signal. Then it's back to the daily routine of following the slow-moving manatee, taking notes about its travel patterns, where it stops, how long it spends in each place. The researchers take note of exact locations with a GPS receiver and record information about the water, such as temperature. At one point Jeferson pulls a disk out of his gear bag; it's an instrument used to measure the turbidity of the water. He lowers the disk with a fishing line until it disappears, and then he measures the length of the rope, marking the depth of the water when the disk disappeared from sight.

Fernando looks at the water and waits for Anama to surface. "I want to see these guys," he says. He half expects Anama to rise any moment, perhaps to get fed, the way he was fed in Manaus for so many years. Fernando teases, "He could jump right out of the water, so overjoyed to see us! You know, Free Willy!" This of course is a joke, because the last animal on earth to jump out of the water with that kind of dramatic energy would be a manatee.

Fernando measures the temperature of the water.

This Amazonian manatee (below) is in a tank; all you see are the nostrils. An Amazonian manatee can be even more difficult to spot in the river.

Fernando checks the group's location on the GPS.

As the boat races up a very narrow tributary called Rio Branquinho, Fernando says that he and his assistants will follow these manatees for another year or two, depending on how long the batteries in the belts last. He confers with his two young assistants about how best to follow the animals. The idea, Fernando tells the two young men, is to stay in the area as long as possible with a small wooden canoe, to try to collect the feces to see what the manatees are eating at this time of year. He also encourages them to mark even the subtlest of animal movements, because in this season the river is getting very shallow very fast; he is curious to see what the manatees will do in the dropping water. In fact, he is somewhat worried that the manatees, not accustomed to such seasonal variation in water depths, might get stranded in the forest.

The banks are very close together, but the pilot is running the boat fast. Suddenly he kills the motor, and the boat drifts up to a wall of jungle. Heads turn because everyone hears the sound of a cat, or is it a bird? No, it's only Fernando himself, smiling. When he is happy, he likes to make bird and cat sounds, meowing and whistling through his teeth. Diogo laughs. Everyone can tell Fernando is happy—in spite of his worries about Puru. He loves being away from the traffic of Manaus, way up these little rivers. Like so many scientists, he loves fieldwork. Fernando, his wife says, makes bird and cat sounds only when he's happy. And happy he does seem as the little group follows the chirping of the telemetric receiver, trying to find out why Puru's signal has not moved in a month.

Fernando especially loves being out of the lab and in the middle of nature. Here, his shirt reads FRIEND OF THE MANATEE.

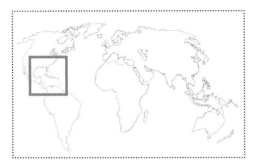

Florida and the Gulf

It is vital that scientists doing aerial surveys have great communication with their pilots. John (right) and Paul have worked together for decades.

A couple thousand miles away, it's a chilly winter morning in central Florida when Dr. John Reynolds, a manatee expert at Mote Marine Laboratory in Sarasota, hops into a small Cessna airplane with his pilot, Paul Gallizzi, to begin an all-day aerial survey to count manatees around the state. He studies both the Florida manatee, *Trichechus manatus latirostris*, and the Antillean manatee or Caribbean manatee (*Trichechus manatus manatus*), found in waters throughout the Caribbean and off the coast of Mexico. They are the two subspecies of the West Indian manatee. John has been conducting these winter surveys for thirty years; Paul has been his pilot for twenty of those because, as John puts it, "Paul is fun, he places high priority on safety, and he can turn on a dime, which is essential for counting manatees gathered in warm-water discharges."

John grew up outside Baltimore, Maryland, amid farmland and cow pastures. He did a lot of fishing in the ponds, collected snakes and frogs, and went crabbing with his dad in Chesapeake Bay. He got a degree in biological oceanography with a focus on wildlife management of marine mammals. John, like Fernando, loves fieldwork.

Donning their headphones, Paul and John lift off into the darkness near Tampa, heading straight for the eastern horizon. John has spent more than fifteen hundred hours in small planes surveying Florida manatees; he has conducted more of these surveys than anyone else over the past thirty years, and he knows exactly how to be patient and pick the perfect days—a mix of prolonged or intensely cold temperatures, sunny skies, and light winds. At such times, manatees gather in warm-water spots, such as power plant discharge areas and natural springs. With the light winds and clear

Dr. Reynolds has spent many hundreds of hours in single-engine, high-winged aircraft, counting manatees and other marine mammals.

skies, the animals will be much more visible than usual, enabling an accurate count. Today is such a day: windless, sunny, cold, and perfect.

Why conduct surveys during a cold snap? And why power plants? Manatees are susceptible to cold and hypothermia, a condition that occurs when body temperature has been lowered to a dangerous level. Manatees exhibit signs of stress when they are subjected for extended periods to water temperatures much below 68° Fahrenheit (20° Celsius). During the cold periods in south Florida, manatees congregate and find refuge either in the warm 72°F water of natural springs such as Crystal River, or in the warm-water discharges from big power plants up and down both Florida coasts.

Fernando has the gargantuan task of counting Amazonian manatees in murky water over a range too vast to survey, but the clear waters of Florida offer a perfect opportunity for John to count these mildly social creatures, which bunch together in winter, sometimes hundreds in one place. (Scientists gauge a total count of about forty-five hundred manatees in the whole state.) John has counted more than five hundred animals at one power plant. Today he will count

manatees at seven plants, taking notes as Paul spins the plane round and round, tipping one wing straight down at the water. John has no problem with airsickness, but he's taken a lot of people up who have returned to land pretty green in the face.

A Florida manatee rises to the surface to breathe.

Seeing manatees from a plane is a remarkable experience. John says, "You're only seven hundred feet above the water, and you can see them rise to breathe and interact with one another. You see the moms and the calves beside them, many with boat scars on their back."

John is aware that these surveys don't tell us all we need to know in order to establish the conservation status of this, or any, marine mammal, but they do help. "We determine the status of manatee populations from some rather limited information," he admits. "In Florida we do aerial surveys and photo identification and mark-and-recapture modeling."

A manatee calf suckles at its mother's breast, which is located on the flipper.

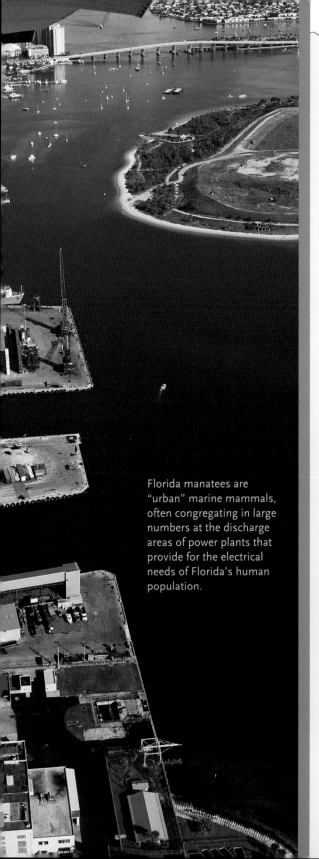

Florida manatees are "urban" marine mammals, often congregating in large numbers at the discharge areas of power plants that provide for the electrical needs of Florida's human population.

Mark and recapture is a method commonly used in ecology to estimate population size. Scientists capture and tag a set number of animals, release them, and then go back to the same study area to capture the same number of manatees again. Based on how many of those individuals have tags, scientists can hypothesize, or make an educated guess, as to what the overall population of the study area is.

How does John actually count animals during a population survey? Years of practice, he says. Today a few of the power plants have gone off line, like the one at Riviera Beach. Even so, he notices about 180 manatees at the Riviera plant waiting for the warm water to start flowing. When he lands, he will relay this information to the Florida Power and Light Company, an organization that has placed a priority on manatee conservation for many years and wants to be sure the animals are not in jeopardy. The power company, because of John's call later that day, will actually turn on its plant for a few days, just to keep the manatees safe.

John sees the larger picture, not just from the air but also from his vantage point as chairman of the United States Marine Mammal Commission for the past two decades. The commission was created under the Marine Mammal Protection Act of 1972, and its primary duties involve providing oversight for conservation of all marine mammals and

Manatees are easy to spot and count in the discharge zone at Florida Power and Light Company's Riviera power plant along Lake Worth.

their habitats in U.S. waters. Appointed to the position by President George H. W. Bush in 1991, John has had to testify before Congress on many subjects relating to marine mammal research and conservation. He has also served as the cochair of the Sirenia Specialist Group at the IUCN, the organization that maintains the Red List.

"Because we can actually count them and do long-term trend analyses using photo identification and mark-recapture modeling," John says, "we have a pretty good idea about the status of manatees here in Florida. But in Brazil and West Africa, this isn't the case. One Amazon researcher told me that in her entire life she's probably seen ten Amazonian manatees in the river . . . ever! They're impossible to survey down there." Scientists like Fernando Rosas rely heavily on local information, often on stories told by the very people who hunt manatees to eat. "Also," John continues, "the other two species of manatee live in murky water in vast and uncharted regions. So how do you get an impression for status if you can't find the animals and they're still being killed in unknown numbers for food?" It's a good question.

When Paul lands the plane at the tiny airport near Tampa, John says, "That was a good day. More than a thousand manatees." The total number of adults today was 1,057; calves, 61. Once, he managed to count 2,233 manatees at nine locations. In his three decades of conducting winter power plant surveys, he's counted more than a thousand animals

Manatees and kayakers often use the same quiet waterways.

only a few times. These are high numbers in optimal conditions, but counting manatees is only part of what John does to establish the conservation status of the Florida manatee species.

Back in his office at Mote, John says, "One of the things manatee experts are now working on, which has previously been poorly understood, is the health of the species." He wants to include the very important attribute of an animal's health in what determines the conservation status. "Too often this criterion is not considered when establishing conservation status."

Using the information about what constitutes a healthy manatee, John explains as he leans back in his chair, can also help scientists better deal with stranded or sick animals. To this end, John has worked with manatee expert Dr. Benjamin Morales on stranded manatees in Mexico. "Once you understand what's normal for a manatee or any species, then you have a better

In Mexico, captured manatees are lugged ashore, where they can be weighed, measured, and examined. Blood, urine, and other samples are taken and a tag is attached to each animal. All hands are expected to help carry the thousand-pound animals. Dr. Morales (front left) and Dr. Reynolds (front right) do their share of the work.

Two Florida manatees swim together—but one swims upside down!

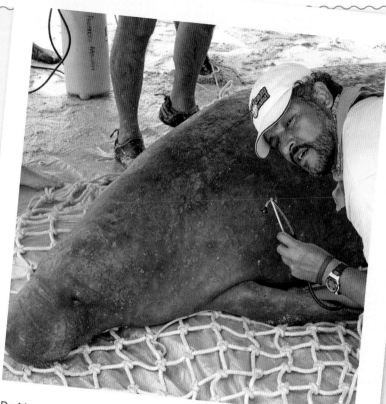

Dr. Marco Benitez, a veterinarian, works closely with Dr. Morales to conduct a thorough physical examination on captured manatees as a part of a health assessment project.

But this is an incomplete picture for determining the actual status of a species. It doesn't take into account the quality of the animals. Are they mostly males? "If so," he says, "they're not going to reproduce. That's not a very healthy situation for the species. Are they all very elderly animals that are past their reproductive period? That's not good for the species either. Are they sick animals? Until now we have had no way of knowing the answers to these questions. But that is changing. New advances in something called biomarker analysis promise a much better way of determining status."

John thinks we are on the verge of a breakthrough for conservation biology—for establishing the real conservation status of a manatee, or of any animal for that matter. And it comes down not to surveys, but to chemistry. Studies have identified levels of contaminants (poisons, such as pesticides) in tissues of marine mammals, including manatees, but these studies typically fail to provide the real answers that decision makers want and need, such as what effects

chance of understanding what's abnormal, and you can address the problem the animal faces, whether it's internal or in the ecosystem, the habitat in which it lives. That's the importance of knowing the health of animals.

"Typically, we have determined status in only two ways: we go out and count how many animals are swimming around, and we watch how many have washed up on the beaches," says John.

Scientists and assistants in Mexico have completed their examination of a manatee and prepare to return it to the water.

those contaminants have on the health, reproductive ability, and survival of the animals.

This new science being developed in labs in the United States is beginning to help us better understand the real health of individual animals and of the species they belong to. Initial blood tests on manatees are showing that it might well be possible to tell just how fertile a female is. "If we can measure the fertility of mammals of all types, not just manatees, this would be incredible for captive breeding programs and for zoos, as well as for all wild conservation programs." And most important, gauging the fertility of females in a population will definitely give us a better idea than mere population counts of that species' conservation status.

During manatee health assessments, team members each have a role so that sampling will occur as efficiently as possible. In this photo Bob Bonde prepares to draw blood while Artie Wong conducts an electrocardiogram to study the manatee's heart rate during capture.

To protect both the manatee and the scientists from the strong Mexican sun, a makeshift shelter is erected on the beach every time an animal is captured and handled.

Research

John Reynolds agrees with what Fernando Rosas has said of the captive Amazonian manatees. It is very important to spend time with the animals in order to understand them. "This is difficult to do with wild manatees," John says, "because they can swim in excess of twenty miles per hour in short bursts and are quite secretive when they want to be."

Florida manatees live in close proximity to very dense human populations, and yet in most parts of the state their populations are increasing. The Florida manatee is certainly among the best-studied marine mammals in the world, in part, John says, because there has been a team approach. They are studied in the wild by many scientists, and they are also studied in great detail in captivity. All this science in Florida will help us understand aspects of the other two species. At Mote Marine Labo-

ratory, for instance, where John works, two resident manatees, Hugh and Buffett, go through scientific trials and tests every morning before Mote opens to the public.

Years of studies on Hugh and Buffett have provided great insights into many aspects of manatee physiology, including

Mote Marine Laboratory is home to two captive-born manatees, Hugh and Buffett, who nuzzle John Reynolds's hands in hopes of something to eat.

the role of the tiny hairs all over their bodies. These are sensory hairs—used for detecting subtle movements in water. Much of the time manatees live in cloudy water where vision is not a useful sense. They have great hearing, but one question scientists are trying to answer is how they navigate in murky water. One possibility is through sensory touch, the ability to find and detect movement. This manatee sense of active touch, experiments show, is equivalent to the sensitivity we have on our index fingers. In one recent study, researchers at

Manatee trainers at Mote use food as a reward for when the manatees are put through various tests.

A manatee's whiskers can be used in ways the author's whiskers cannot—they are very sensitive to changes in the water.

At Mote Marine Laboratory, trainers work daily with Hugh and Buffett.

Mote learned that manatees can somehow discriminate as well as humans can sense and read Braille with their fingers. And scientists think this sensitivity may come through the hairs all over their bodies.

"So what is the relationship between the science that we do and actually conserving the animals?" John asks. Then he answers his own question: "The sensory biology tells us how they get around in their environment and what they perceive. If you can understand what they hear, then you can understand whether they're able to detect boats and, if so, at what distances." Boats in Florida kill a lot of West Indian manatees. But if scientists can understand what a manatee can and can't hear, and at what distances, then conservation managers can set policy for speeds of boats in certain manatee habitats. "In other words," John says, "science informs conservation."

"A manatee is an amazing animal," he says, "a hodgepodge of mammalian adaptations. It has things no other mammal has. The arrangements of organs and tissues are just weird." John cowrote a paper called "Diaphragm Structure and Function in the Florida Manatee," which describes how manatees let gas out to maintain neutral buoyancy. Basically—the importance of passing gas! John says in a serious scientific tone, "A manatee has gas in the lungs, gas in the intestines from all the plants it eats. And it has this immensely elongated and powerful diaphragm that can pressurize that gas and put it into areas of its body—larger and smaller containers, if you will. If you watch a manatee you can see it rise and fall making no external movement at all. We think it is regulating this internally by regulating distribution of the gas in the guts. Every now and then they produce methane because of all that plant eating. In other words, they fart as an additional mechanism of regulating buoyancy." Watching manatees in captivity on a regular basis has helped

Dr. Gordon Bauer is a biologist at Mote specializing in animal sensory processes, cognition, and behavior. He is currently studying the vision, touch, hearing, and chemical senses of manatees.

While Buffett goes through tests in his tank at Mote, one trainer holds Hugh's flippers and feeds him. His training will be next.

John come to this conclusion about manatee flatulence.

In studying the biology of an animal, it is important to be able to recognize individuals, their reproductive cycles, their behavior, and their relationships to one another. Unlike in the murky waters of the Amazon and Africa, scientists in coastal Florida are able to identify individual animals in the clear water. "The scars from boat collisions on the backs of manatees help with ID," says John. "Some have been hit up to fifty times, so they really do take a beating. But they're still out there, living perhaps sixty years or longer in a normal life span. Although they often survive boat hits,

This Florida manatee has its mouth open. It may be burping!

A close-up of propeller scars on the back of a Florida manatee.

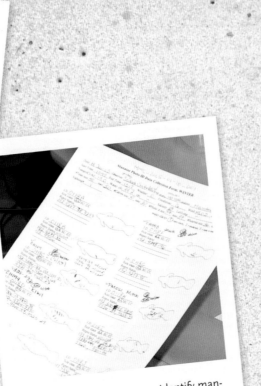

Scientists use these forms to identify manatees based on scars and other markings.

these collisions probably affect their reproductive ability. A female that gets hit multiple times by a boat or propeller probably isn't going to ovulate for a while. It will put every bit of energy into recovery, not into reproduction. This, the health of reproducing females, should be taken into account when defining manatees' status." Studying the scars on the manatees and following up on these animals year after year in a mark-and-recapture study, with particular attention to adult female survival, helps scientists understand large behavioral patterns.

John's manatee team identifies individual animals and, along with the state and federal governments, maintains a statewide catalog of Florida manatees. Follow-ing the behavior of manatees through photo identification teaches scientists individual life histories—how often they breed, where they migrate, what triggers these migrations, what habitats certain groups prefer, and so on. For example, females choose different habitats than males choose. "In fact," John says, "females with calves use the Sarasota Bay area differently from all the other demographic groups of manatees. They're going into protected areas, for instance, much more than the manatee population in general." John's team learns about this

The veterinarian Marco Benitez from Africam Safari Zoo evaluates the health condition of a manatee captured in Chetumal Bay. Researchers will take biological information, then track its movements off the Caribbean coasts of Mexico and Belize.

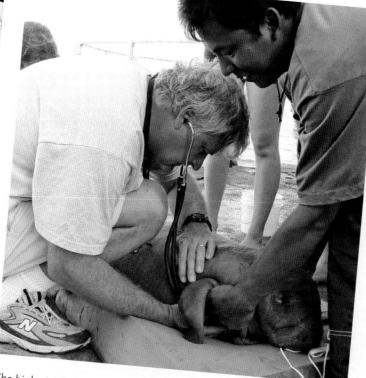

The biologist Bob Bonde leans over a captured baby Antillean manatee with a stethoscope, listening to its heart rate.

from photo identification, following the animals year after year.

Another way scientists in Florida study manatees is by tagging them, which is similar to what Fernando is doing in the Amazon, except here scientists use satellite tags. They mark the manatee with an orange or a blue belt around its peduncle. The transmitter itself, in a canister attached to a tube that trails behind the manatee, broadcasts different frequencies to track the animal's whereabouts and what habitat it is in, even when it is underwater. The belt has a five-foot tether with breakable links, so if the animal is within five or six feet of the surface, this little canister with a battery in it stays on the surface and is detectable by the satellite.

"You have to be really clever to catch a manatee," says John, smiling. "You need a clever bit of bait. We use a hose with fresh water coming out of it. When an animal comes up and drinks out of the hose, researchers walk the net up behind it and pull it up on the beach." (It is illegal in Florida to "water" manatees, because it brings them in close proximity to boats. Many people in Florida do it, but it should be discouraged because it puts manatees in harm's

way. The Mote has a special permit that allows them to do this in order to conduct scientific research.) Researchers, including those at Mote, also net manatees without using hoses, at places they normally gather in winter.

Manatees are immense and strong in spite of their blubbery appearance, and they weigh up to thirty-six hundred pounds. "They are pretty harmless unless they roll on you," says John. That's not a joke. John has a buddy whose leg broke in five places when he got caught in the net and fell under a manatee that rolled backwards.

There are a lot of tagged animals out there. So what can they tell us? Mostly it's all about movement. And specifically for conservation purposes, the information helps scientists understand what habitats the manatees prefer, and those habitats can then be protected. Using something called satellite telemetry, a scientist gets several hits a day that he or she can document to find out when the manatees move into the warm water or

Scientists capture a manatee with a net in Crystal River, Florida.

A team of scientists examines a captured Antillean manatee in Puerto Rico. The strap over the top of the manatee is for restraint while the animal is out of the water. It is also used to roll the manatee safely.

go out to beds of sea grass. The behaviors of organisms that are inaccessible or difficult for humans to follow can be studied with the aid of satellite telemetry, a satellite-based location and data-collection system that allows a transmitter, attached to an animal, to be located to within 350 meters. This transmitter "talks" to the receiver in the satellite. Scientists can map the routes manatees are using for travel. If they go along a certain narrow canal, for instance, that

might be an area to protect during the migratory season. Again, that's how science is used to help conserve animals.

John explains a bit more. "With the use of tags, we also learn a lot about habitat preferences. The Florida Manatee Sanctuary Act says that the state of Florida is a manatee sanctuary. Would the citizens of Florida like it if we prohibited all human activities in the waters of the whole state? Not likely. Many people would complain. They would say it was unfair. And it would be. So we try to find some balance. If you let the manatees tell you what areas they like, by tagging them and watching their movements, then you can protect those areas of heavy manatee use and allow humans to do things in other areas." It's a way to compromise so that manatees and humans can live together.

John's office at Mote is crammed with souvenirs he's collected from around the globe. Pins on the world map on his wall show all the places he's traveled. He gets excited when he says things like "The Serengeti in East Africa is the most amazing place for wildlife in the world." His finger moves across the Atlantic to Mexico, and he says, "I love Mexico"—finger moving northeast—"and the Caribbean . . . I like Brazil a lot." His finger waves over large expanses of the planet. "I like the Japanese. I guess I like people." It is clear that wherever he travels, he marvels at the dedicated peo-

Low-tech approaches work fine! For Dr. Morales and his colleagues, ingenuity and muscle can provide good substitutes for expensive boats and other gear.

ple he is lucky enough to meet—people who share his vision of using science to inform and promote effective conservation decisions for wildlife.

Although his early work focused primarily on manatees (he's written several books, book chapters, and many articles on the sirenians), he now spends much of his time traveling the world, helping other countries come up with marine mammal action plans and commissions like the one he chairs in the United States. He was an advisor to the Caribbean regional office of the United Nations Environment Programme for the development of a Caribbean-wide Marine Mammal Action Plan designed to promote conservation and science for whales, dolphins, and manatees of the region. He is helping specific islands and nations conserve and restore their ecosystems and is currently working on projects in the Dominican Republic, Mexico, Curaçao, and Guadeloupe.

John, perhaps more than any other manatee scientist in the field today, keeps his eyes on the big picture. Even as he travels the world as commissioner for marine mammals and advisor to other countries, he always finds time to continue his yearly aerial surveys in Florida. He sees the limits of this kind of traditional technique in establishing a species' conservation status and he knows that in order to get a real sense of how the manatee, or any species, is faring in the wild, it will be crucial to accurately measure the health of the species, something that now seems exciting and possible with new techniques in chemistry and chemical analysis that he facilitates with Dana Wetzel, Benjamin Morales, and Bill Roudebush, among others.

John Reynolds loves his job, loves to go out into the field to collect data. A few years ago, when he was collecting samples from seals and whales on the North Slope of Alaska, the Iñupiaq Eskimos gave him an Eskimo name. "They gave me an etched piece of baleen with my Eskimo name on it," he says, pointing. "It means Swimming Walrus."

For the moment, John stands in front of the world map on his wall. Perhaps thinking of all the places he has been and all the places he'd still like to see, he smiles, a man with a full and exciting life.

John Reynolds standing in front of the world map in his office.

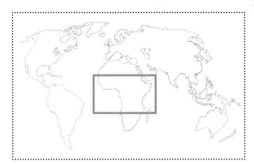

Africa

Halfway across the world from both John and Fernando, biologist Lucy Keith Diagne has been crisscrossing Africa for the past ten years, exploring the third manatee species, *Trichechus senegalensis*. She's been talking to fishermen and manatee hunters, collecting tissue and bone samples for DNA analysis, and helping researchers, managers of parks, and government officials get together to begin programs that will not only give us an idea where African manatees are and in what numbers, but also help conserve them. One of her goals has been to create a network of all the people studying and working with manatees in Africa so that these researchers can begin to work together and share their knowledge. Now, thanks in part to Lucy's hard work, collaborators from no fewer than nineteen countries are participating in the African "manatee network"!

Lucy has studied a wide range of endangered species, including green sea turtles, Hawaiian monk seals, and Florida and Antillean manatees. She was born for this kind of work—the rugged travel of long days and nights out in the bush. Her father is an ornithologist with a specialty in the birds of Central and South America, so Lucy grew up loving wildlife and the outdoors. One day when she was young, she learned about manatees in school, and she came home to tell her parents she was going to save them. "I grew up in the Northeast, in rural New Jersey, and always knew I wanted to be a biologist. For a while I worked with penguins, but while working with them in Antarctica, I fell in love with seals, so I began pursuing jobs with marine mammals. I worked with seals for a few years and then worked with manatees in Florida and Belize for six years before I came to Africa."

Lucy provides one-on-one training in manatee field techniques and data recording for a Gabonese biologist at N'dogo Lagoon.

This mud-covered African manatee was rescued from the Navel tributary in eastern Senegal. This species is similar to the Florida manatee, except it is generally smaller and the eyes protrude more.

A Theory of How African Manatees Got to Africa

Lucy's doctoral research proved that the African manatee evolved from the West Indian manatee. This was accomplished by comparing DNA samples Lucy collected from African manatees to samples previously collected from West Indian and Amazonian manatees. Each DNA sample was compared to all the others, and finally produced a special graph, known as a "phylogenetic tree." The tree shows how all the manatees are related to each other and when the species separated. Lucy's analyses showed that African manatees are most closely related to West Indian manatees that today live along the Atlantic coast of Venezuela, Guyana, French Guyana, and Brazil, and that the two species separated approximately 3.5 to 4 million years ago.

Armed with that information, Lucy researched environmental conditions 3 to 4 million years ago. At that time, known as the Pliocene, the continents were in approximately the same positions as today. The formation of the Isthmus of Panama closed off the Central American Seaway and caused large-scale oceanic changes around the globe. The temperature of all the world's oceans increased to an average of three degrees celsius warmer than today and currents that primarily circulated east to west mostly weakened. However, another current strengthened: the North Equatorial Countercurrent (NECC) originates in the Atlantic Ocean near French Guyana and Brazil and moves from west to east, reaching the African continent between Senegal and Sierra Leone. It strengthens during warmer time periods and therefore may have been stronger during the Pliocene.

Trichechids (all the manatee species) are thought to have evolved in South America, and they likely moved into the Caribbean during this time. They could have then been caught up in the NECC and transported to Africa. Over time, the manatees that arrived in Africa and spread out along the coast and up rivers became a distinct species, *Trichechus senegalensis*.

Studying manatees in Africa has been difficult for many reasons, including the vast and remote nature of some areas. African manatees range over an area that covers twenty-one countries—some of them beset by complex politics—where there was vry little previous work, mostly interviewing people and trying to get a handle on the status of the manatees. As

Lucy Keith Diagne leads a class discussion on the manatee using an educational coloring and activity book she designed in French at the school in Sette Cama, Gabon.

Lucy puts it, "Who you talk to and what they know is very important. Interviews are heavily relied on because there is so little recorded information on this species, so local knowledge is a good place to start. Not everything an interviewee says is necessarily true, but information gleaned from fishermen and hunters is added to our overall knowledge, and slowly we get a better picture."

Lucy, having spent more than seven years in Gabon, also began studies in Angola and Senegal. The IUCN Red List designation of Vulnerable for the African manatee is based on very limited information, so she and her colleagues from many countries are beginning to fill in the blank spots. Now that the network is set up and collecting data regularly in ten countries throughout the range, it is hoped that the conservation status of this species will become clearer.

When Lucy describes her passion for her work, her voice is elevated and she talks fast, almost as if she might be overwhelmed at any minute—but overwhelmed in a good way. It's the sound of true excitement, like that of someone stumbling upon a lost treasure. This scientifically untapped region holds one of the world's three manatee species, and it is believed that there may be more African manatees than Florida manatees. The range of the African manatee is huge (wider than the width of the United States), and in certain places, such as Gabon and Senegal, the species is seen and reported a lot more commonly than ever before. Lucy is the first

Women paddle a traditional canoe on the Congo River near the village of Luamba, Angola.

While conducting boat surveys for manatees, Lucy takes detailed notes in a waterproof field notebook, including habitat type, plant species, any signs of manatee feeding, and environmental data.

been analyzed from all African manatees. Genetics is an important tool used by scientists to determine where different populations of animals exist, how closely related populations and different species are to each other, and to estimate how many individuals are in a population. The manatee physiologist Dr. Bob Bonde, Lucy's friend and colleague, urged her to collect samples while on her travels, and he later convinced her to do genetics analysis as part of her Ph.D. research. Lucy also works with other biologists to take basic health information on the manatees she locates, so they can learn for the first time what a healthy African manatee looks like. This isn't yet known for the species.

People are still some of the most important resources Lucy has in her survey work for finding the elusive African manatee and for determining the number of animals that exist in any part of any country. One of the first things

to admit, however, that there are as yet no accurate abundance estimates for the species anywhere at a countrywide level, much less regionally. She thinks that in places with low human density, such as Gabon, the species appears to be thriving, and that these are the best places for conservation efforts. There is so much to learn.

When Lucy began working in Africa, less than thirty genetic samples had ever

Lucy Keith Diagne interviews a fisherman in Cap Esterias in northern Gabon. People in this community do not hunt manatees, because they know they are long-lived and have few offspring. This man's grandfather once found a manatee caught alive in a net. He kept it for a week to observe it, then set it free.

she does when she starts working in a new place is to go out onto the rivers to talk to local hunters and fishermen and villagers. "It's kinda fun," she says, "because every day you learn something new." She pauses, her face looking a little sad. "The hard thing is when you learn that ninety-five manatees have been killed by hunters on one river alone."

Conservation in Africa has to take into consideration the socioeconomic and cultural situations in developing countries, because effective conservation will not happen without addressing these issues. When Lucy talks to people in the field, she interviews them simply to determine whether manatees are in an area. She's getting a relative measure of how many are seen by locals (none, very few, occasionally seen, or seen every day). "Then I follow up with my own

boat surveys to determine where manatees are, seasonality, habitat use, and so forth. I cannot make people stop killing them myself, but I collect information that will help wildlife law enforcement agencies stop illegal hunting." Hunting is a complex issue, she realizes, since people are poor and they need protein. Hunting is their livelihood (in places where hunting occurs), so people need other economic alternatives if we are

Local children in a village on the Sereia Peninsula, Soyo, Angola, gather around to listen when Lucy discusses manatees with village chiefs and fishermen.

On the Sereia peninsula at the mouth of the Congo River, channels of water with huge mangroves provide food and quiet areas for African manatees to live in.

going to stop hunting. Just talking to them would not help, she says. "What I do tell people I want to stop hunting is this: 'I only want there to be enough manatees for the future, for your children and grandchildren. I would have no problem with hunting, as long as we can make sure there are enough manatees to survive for the future, but right now, we don't have enough information to ensure that.'" This approach works, she says. "[It] changes their perception of what I'm trying to do and makes them much more willing to talk to me about realistic options."

Lucy made three trips up the Congo

River in Angola to do some basic work—boat and interview surveys. In the boat surveys Lucy looked for manatees, studied their habitat, observed plants for signs of feeding. She tallied up the number and size of villages in the area and gauged the human impact on the manatees. "I also stop at villages along the route and talk to everyone I can about where the manatees are seen, and how often. I ask questions like, Do they think there were more in past years? Do they see babies, groups? What kinds of behavior in the animals have they noted? Do they know what they eat? Do they hunt them, or do they know a hunter? Are manatees traditionally respected? Are there local legends about them? These are all standardized questions asked the same way at each village (the actual question form was developed by Buddy Powell years ago) so that responses can be compared within an area as well as across different regions and countries."

The villagers were very friendly. "They don't see a lot of white women traveling up the river," she says. They told her that they see manatees almost every day. Lucy herself has spent many hours on different parts of the river, quiet-

Sebastian Domingo killed an average of three African manatees a week for thirty years, using harpoons with floats attached and a wooden canoe.

ly drifting and waiting, hoping to spot one. "The more I traveled up the Congo exploring new tributaries, all great habitats for manatees, the more I realized that manatees have an enormous network of mostly undisturbed mangrove and rainforest channels, with relatively few villages and very few motorized boats, so it's no wonder that they have managed to survive so well there," she said. Thick vegetation overhangs the river, providing perfect food and hiding places. She spotted a monitor lizard and many hippos, but only one manatee,

which spent a whole hour near her boat.

She came to a small village called N'Tutu, where she found out that a well-known manatee hunter named Sebastian Domingo recently had died from an infection in his leg. She had met him the year before. He was a very interesting man, with a great knowledge about manatees in the area, their behavior, their movement patterns, but, as she put it, "of course he was also killing several manatees a week." Now that Mr. Domingo, the only hunter in an area of the river that stretches for forty kilometers (twenty-five miles), was gone, Lucy hoped the manatees would be safer. She admired the wealth of local and historical knowledge of manatees that a man like Mr. Domingo retained. He had known about their habitat use and their distribution in the area, and she would have liked to talk to him a lot more, especially since he was happy to share his stories. But she also knew that he would never stop hunting. Luckily, the younger generation in the village didn't seem interested in taking up the hunt.

When she arrived at Mr. Domingo's hut, she found his harpoons. Then she

Sebastian Domingo's hut at N'Tutu, Angola.

The herpetologist Warren Klein helped Lucy collect manatee bones at N'Tutu after Sebastian Domingo passed away. A herpetologist studies amphibians.

found something amazing behind the cooking area—manatee bones scattered everywhere, some fresh, some old. She ended up collecting 154 bones—a biologist's treasure-trove of genetic information for her research—without doubt the largest number of African manatee bones ever collected, representing a minimum of thirteen individual animals.

The day after her incredible find, she cut bone samples with a hacksaw, washing its blade with bleach after each cut to avoid contaminating the next sample. Bob Bonde had advised her exactly where to take samples on each bone

type in order to have the best possibility of getting good DNA for analysis. The job took two days, two hacksaw blades, and a lot of plastic cling wrap. Joined by another biologist and an Angolan biology student, Lucy labeled each bone with a unique ID number, photographed it next to a measuring tape (to document size), and entered each into a database that described basic information such as the type of bone (rib, sternum, etc.). The

Lucy with the 101 bones collected at Sebastian Domingo's village after he passed away. This is the largest number of manatee bones ever collected for genetic analysis for the species. These bones represent a minimum of thirteen individuals, but could include many more; genetic analysis may allow scientists to determine the exact number. An additional fifty bones were later found in the same area by the hunter's wife, who gave them to Lucy.

bones will be used primarily for genetic analysis.

Before leaving the Congo River and Angola, Lucy arranged with her longtime translator, João Barbosa, to contact Mr. Domingo's two sons to see if she could acquire their father's harpoons, so that no one would be tempted to take up the business of manatee hunting. Manatee meat brings in a much higher price on the market than fish, and as she has written in her blog, "Because Mr. Domingo was the only hunter in such a large area, it would have a big impact on manatee conservation to get these harpoons 'off the street' and into a museum where they belong!"

Angola manatee hunter Sebastian Domingo's cooking hut at N'Tutu, where manatee meat was smoked. More than 120 manatee bones were found in the mangroves behind this hut.

African manatee bones found in N'Tutu. Lucy brought them back to her base in Soyo and carefully numbered and documented each bone, then cut out samples that she will use to do genetic analysis at the University of Florida.

Lucy Keith Diagne examines a manatee harpoon (with float attached) in N'Tutu, Angola, in August 2008. This harpoon belonged to Sebastian Domingo, who had passed away the previous week.

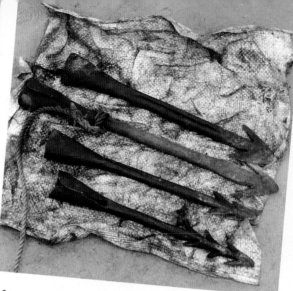

African manatee hunter's harpoon tips, Togo.

In her wide-ranging travels, Lucy has found manatees in places she would never have believed—far inland from the coast, up rivers and streams, and even in deserts.

In early 2009 she and biologists from four other countries drove across Senegal to the edge of the Sahara Desert to rescue ten manatees

A typical house in the Sahel of eastern Senegal.

trapped above new dams on the Senegal River. It was a dusty day-and-a-half drive through small villages, windy and bone-dry—the last place on earth most people would expect to find manatees.

During the rainy season, when the river is flooding, local people dam the many small tributaries to conserve water for growing crops as the water recedes. "These dams are permanent," Lucy says. "Two were recently installed, and at least one more is under construction, so the problem will continue, although there are hopeful signs that a committee of local and national agencies will be created to find solutions." The water was falling fast in the remaining pools, and the manatees were going to die if they didn't get any help. In one channel—about 14 meters wide (46 feet) and 600 meters long (656 yards) and maybe 1.5 meters deep (5 feet)—she saw five noses in the milk-chocolate water. A guard had been hired to watch the manatees. Some vil-

Ali San, a local man from Navel, Senegal, was hired to guard the African manatees trapped in the tributary for several weeks while preparations could be made to rescue, tag, and relocate them back to the main Senegal River. Ali San stayed with the manatees day and night, camping by the river and providing corn husks for them to eat, since there was no food available as the water level fell.

lagers believe the breath of the manatee can kill a person, and they might have wanted to kill these trapped beasts before they could be rescued and transported back to the main channel of the river.

After scouting the site and planning a rescue, Lucy instructed two collaborators on how to assemble the satellite tags she planned to put on some of the manatees to track their movements. This was the first time satellite tags were ever used to study African manatees. Any data they could get would be very important, because so little is known about their migration patterns or their habitat requirements, or even how many manatees there are in the Senegal River itself.

At the dam, workers cleared a path on the hillside so that Lucy and the other scientists could back a trailer attached to a tractor down to the water's edge. The next morning, fishermen entered the waterway with nets and captured three manatees. "It was nerve-racking," Lucy says, "because the fishermen just sort of 'wing it,' and not much is coordinated." Hundreds of onlookers descended on the manatees when they were finally brought to shore. Some people were just curious; others wanted to hurt the manatees.

The Navel dam in eastern Senegal is one of several new dams designed to hold back water for crops during the eight-month dry season in this desert region. In the rainy season, water flows in from the Senegal River over the top of the dam (through the openings seen below the road), and manatees swim in to feed on the flooded grasses and trees. Unfortunately, as the water falls, it also traps manatees behind the dam. Four manatees have died at the dam itself, trapped against the grills in strong currents that don't allow them to the surface to breathe.

Police officers protected the operation, but the crowd was almost out of control. Lucy says, "I have to say, I've never experienced such chaos during manatee captures. Caught up in the hysteria of the crowd, people literally ran up to the trailer, grabbing at our clothes and arms, trying to fling themselves in."

As the first two manatees were driven the three kilometers (almost two miles) over the dam and down the road to the release site on the river, Lucy tried to conduct health assessments on the animals inside the trailer. She took basic

An African manatee rests just after capture by fishermen. Three of the five captured manatees were tagged with satellite transmitters so scientists could begin to understand their seasonal movement patterns.

measurements (standard lengths and girths: total straight length, total curvilinear length, axillary girth, umbilical girth, anal girth, and peduncle girth). She also took genetic samples, but not much else. Every time the tractor pulling the trailer stopped, a new crowd descended on the animals. She knew she needed to train the other biologists quickly in how to take samples and how to attach the tracking gear, as most of them had not worked on manatees before. In the end, she did figure out the sex of the animals and got the measurements she needed along with the genetic samples she used in later analyses.

When Lucy returned for the third manatee, it had been loaded onto a pickup truck. She had left it in the shade of a tree with instructions to pour water over it to keep it cool. There was nothing wrong with the manatee; it was perfectly safe from harm, but people were scared that it would die and had already loaded it up on the truck.

Lucy says, "Unlike dolphins, manatees can comfortably stay out of the

Local fishermen put the trapped manatees in nets in the tributary while a crowd watches.

water on land for several hours, as long as they are monitored and kept cool. Their solid rib bones support and protect their internal organs." Lucy and her colleagues transported this one to the river below the dam and tagged it.

The following day, the biologists caught two more, one female and a huge adult male. The male was 290 centimeters (9.5 feet), very big for an African manatee

An African manatee sits in a net before it is relocated to the main Senegal River.

and definitely the largest of the group they captured. The female was 8.5 feet (260 centimeters), a more typical size. They tagged the female. This is the kind of work Lucy does in hopes of learning a lot about the manatees' seasonal movements. She and her colleagues ended up tagging three manatees and were able to track their movements in the Senegal River. "The two males were tagged for four months before they lost their tags due to entanglement in fishing nets," Lucy says. "Luckily the manatees escaped, because the tracking gear is built with specific safety features and will release if the manatee becomes caught. The female manatee was tagged for nine months and during the rainy season, she moved back into the tributary where she was rescued."

Lucy Keith Diagne has a lot of work ahead of her to help establish the conservation status of the African manatee,

Two of the trapped manatees were transported by trailer and released into the main river. During the transport Lucy trained a team of biologists from Senegal, Guinea Bissau, and Spain to take basic measurements and genetic samples, and to fit telemetry gear around the manatees' tails.

and she faces many difficulties. Logistics are complicated; buying basic supplies can take days, and getting to places can take weeks. Travel is always difficult, and she never knows when she might get her next meal. She may hear about a manatee carcass in a certain place but can't get there for two weeks, at which point the carcass is gone. Politics can get in the way. Outbreaks of violence have kept her away from three places in one year alone. The terrain can be very rugged. Living and working in remote places is difficult owing to disease, bugs, and harsh weather. And cultural differences can confound the fieldworker. Often local villagers don't trust outsiders; superstitions and legends about manatees can cloud interviews, and it is often difficult to find reliable field assistants. Language barriers can be a problem, as most rural people speak only local lan-

Lucy fits a manatee tracking belt around the tail of a rescued manatee. Lucy custom builds and fits each belt to the manatee so that it will not impede normal behaviors such as swimming, feeding, and mating. Belts connect to a nylon tether that in turn connects to a floating buoy tag that is towed behind the manatee and sends satellite signals of the manatee's location.

Lucy teaches Spanish researchers how to build manatee satellite tags in Matam, Senegal.

Lucy Keith Diagne photographs African manatees in Lac Cachimba, Gabon, which had the highest sighting frequency for manatees of anywhere Lucy surveyed in Gabon.

guages. Lucy also faces data collection difficulties because equipment is expensive and unwieldy to transport, or it breaks or gets stolen.

Lucy says, "I would say it's almost a shock when something goes right. I'm not complaining at all; it's just a fact of life where I work, and nothing surprises you after a while. You have to really like challenges to do research in Africa." Most of the these problems have nothing to do with the manatees themselves, but Lucy has to get through them just to be able to do her work, which she loves.

She thinks it's possible that she could find more manatees in Africa than scientists had thought existed there, but this doesn't mean these animals aren't extremely threatened by humans, by hunting and development. It's taking a lot of effort to bring people together, to find out where the animals are and how many of them are in each country, and then to set up ways to protect them. Once manatee populations and habitats are identified, conservation measures can follow, such as setting up protected areas and enforcing the protection. Lucy admits that this is an extremely optimistic view, but it has happened in several places in the last few years, so she is convinced it is not beyond the realm of possibility. (Gabon, for instance, established thirteen national parks in 2002, and the first refuge specifically for manatees was established in Lac de Guiers in northern Senegal in 2011.) Increased enforcement to curb poaching would be another big step in all countries, but this will be hard to put into place while people are hungry and poor and governments are corrupt. Lucy knows it will not be easy anywhere in Africa to protect the manatees, but she says, "The more we try, the more likely there will be some bright spots of protection and enforcement in some places, and hopefully that will be enough to protect this wonderful animal for the future."

Lucy Keith Diagne—with a passion for fieldwork and a love of exploring the vast regions of coastal western Africa—definitely has the energy to continue this monumental and exciting task.

Back to the Amazon

In Brazil, Fernando Rosas and his crew continue down the Rio Branquinho. Jeferson assembles the receiver again while the boat floats just off the jungle wall. Then Fernando steps into a small, tippy wooden canoe and Edmar, Chiqúinhó's son, paddles him and the others, one by one, into the forest. There are tapir tracks in the mud. The jungle has a quiet stillness.

Diogo and Jeferson take turns holding the receiver and the antenna over their heads, the electronic chirp coming every few seconds. The signal gets stronger when pointed in certain directions. Often Jeferson or Diogo stops to get a bearing, and then the small group heads off toward the strongest signal, everyone eyeing the ground, hoping to be the first to find Puru's lost belt with the transmitter inside.

For hours it seems as if they've been walking in circles. Fernando thinks that the receiver may be broken, so they

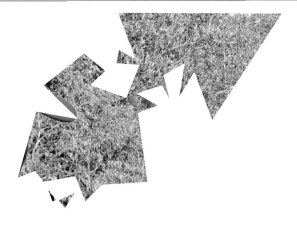

Chiqúinhó's son Edmar paddles Fernando Rosas into the forest in a small wooden canoe.

return to the boat a bit sullen, planning to come back in the morning.

The next day, Edmar leads the scientists back to the same area, through knee-deep water the color of black tea. The telemetric receiver has a new wire to connect the antenna; yesterday there was a loose connection. Diogo again holds it over his head, walking slowly through deepening water toward the strongest chirping sounds.

Fernando looks worried. "Manatees are very sensitive," he says, "with little hairs all over their bodies that measure the water currents. Wild manatees know instinctively that the water drops with the oncoming dry season. But these two animals, raised in captivity, are accustomed to having the water level in their tanks drop all the way down every day when we clean their

Jeferson leads the way through the trees.

Fernando holds up the antenna, happy it is working today.

Fernando up to his knees in water in the flooded forest, looking for Puru.

59

Fernando inspects Puru's collar; it is intact.

The group collects all of Puru's bones . . .

. . . then puts them in a plastic container to study back at INPA.

tanks." Maybe, Fernando is pained to think, Puru got trapped here, not realizing that the water would stay down and not be refilled, as it had been every day for all those years in the manatee tanks in Manaus.

Fernando is now having second thoughts about his choice of rivers for reintroducing these manatees into the wild. He says, "I'm not seeing a lot of grass. That's the trouble with an *igapó*. There is much less grass in this kind of river. Black-water rivers like this one may not be best for manatees. There's food here, yes, but maybe not the best food for these guys." He shakes his head. He

seems to be debating himself. "I do know they can eat the leaves along the banks here. I'm just not sure it will sustain them." (Dr. Best did find that manatees in the Amazon might go months without feeding during the dry season.)

Brown capuchin monkeys, *Macaco prego,* are moving through the trees like giant squirrels. The antenna of the receiver seems to be working well today. Everyone fans out. After less than an hour Jeferson walks straight up to the

collar, which is lying on the jungle floor, and calls out, "I found it!"

Puru's bones are scattered around the forest, gleaming white, picked clean by animals. A sad silence comes over the group of researchers.

Fernando hunts for the skull. "Ah, my baby," he says. "We had you thirteen years. I thought you'd be happy to be back in your house, in the river. Poor guy." Fernando himself had fed Puru from a bottle.

Jeferson, Diogo, and Fernando gather the bones and place them lovingly in a plastic container to bring them back to Manaus for study. Fernando notices some feces nearby, not manatee, so he collects the dung to put under the microscope when he gets back to the city, to see if it might be the animal that ate Puru. "Perhaps a jaguar, *onça*," he says in Portuguese.

He remembers a paper written back in the 1940s about a jaguar that killed a manatee by waiting in a tree over the water. When the manatee was feeding on some plants, the jaguar jumped out of the tree onto the manatee. "Amazing," he says. "That jaguar would have had to spend days and days waiting for the right moment. I've never seen such a thing, but maybe it happens." A jaguar is so big and strong, it could drag a six-hundred-pound manatee for miles. This one probably just dragged the manatee up a little rise in the land to a dry spot, in order to eat it.

"Now the mystery of the lost manatee is solved," Fernando says, though not happily. Everyone watches where he steps. The place has become a sacred site, where one of the only two Amazonian manatees ever raised in captivity and released into the wild found its end. Jeferson sees a mark on a nearby tree

Fernando holds Puru's skull as he talks to his team.

Edmar steadies the canoe for Fernando.

that might have been left by a jaguar. Diogo takes a GPS reading to indicate the exact spot.

Puru's bones are heavy, thick, and dense. This density of bone allows a manatee to stay in the water, achieving neutral buoyancy without the animal having to exert a lot of energy.

Fernando picks up the skull and talks to his assistants about the unique dental configuration of these incredible creatures, seeing the teaching opportunity even in a bad situation. He manages a

laugh, trying to keep things light. Then the cranium is carefully placed on top of the rib bones. Fernando turns toward the river, following Edmar, who, like his dad, knows the way back as if by instinct.

Fernando will save this transmitter and adapt it to fit another animal next year. The plan is to reintroduce two more manatees next March.

Some people have asked Fernando why he isn't planning to release more than two manatees per year, especially since the Manaus tanks are filled to capacity. "Well," he says, "obviously we have to know more. And we'll learn a lot from this experience." He admits that it's important to keep on with this work, to preserve any species not only in captivity but once it is reintroduced to its natural habitat. "We have to start slowly and make sure we are doing the right thing—especially in this age of extinction and human encroachment."

Horseflies—*mutuca,* in Portuguese—buzz wildly back at the boat, where Fernando writes down the coordinates from the GPS. He wants to know exactly where the transmitter was found so he can get the exact distance from where they released the animal. "We can also calculate the distance from here at the boat

to where the transmitter was found," he says. He wants to know how far the transmitter signal can travel through that kind of vegetation. All this information will help with future releases.

Like the other species of manatees, the Amazonian manatee is listed as VU, or vulnerable to extinction, on the IUCN Red List of Threatened Species. But even as Fernando and a handful of other South American manatee scientists learn more about the conservation status of this elusive species, Fernando is trying to do his part in conserving the "ghost of the river" by figuring out how best to release captive manatees back into the wild, where the dangers are many.

As the researchers leave the area, heading downriver for Manaus, the water draining so fast out of the black-water forest that it's as if a plug in a bathtub has been pulled, Puru's remains sit in the plastic container by the outboard motor. Fernando studies the transmitter. The waves grow big on the Rio Negro. The aluminum boat bounces hard, and the container filled with Puru's bones tumbles off the seat and shimmies deep into the boat's stern cavity, out of sight, invisible, the Amazonian manatee secretive even in death.

Fernando begins to whistle.

A close-up of a Florida manatee's fluke as it swims away in Crystal River, Florida.

Manatees at a Glance

General Manatee Facts

• Unlike other marine mammals, such as whales, dolphin, and seals, manatees belong to a group called subungulates. Part of the order Sirenia, they are distantly related to elephants, hyraxes, and aardvarks.

• Manatees have a horizontally flattened fluke and thick skin that can be sparsely covered with hair. A manatee's head and face is generally wrinkled, with whiskers on the snout.

• A manatee has prehensile lips, which means it can grasp vegetation and help guide it into its mouth, the same way an elephant uses its trunk. Manatees are herbivores, which means they eat plants. Manatees eat plants underwater (submerged aquatic vegetation) and plants that overhang the waterways in which they live. Manatees eat a lot, and they eat almost anything. Dr. Reynolds tells his students that if something is green and cannot swim very fast, manatees probably eat it! Manatees commonly feed in shallow waters where vegetation is abundant. It is not uncommon to see them partially out of the water to feed.

• Manatees have two forelimbs, or flippers, which are paddle-shaped, with three or four nails at the tip (except the Amazonian species); the flippers are used to hold food, and guide movement. There are no hind limbs in any of the three species of manatee.

• Manatees communicate through touch, sight, taste, and sound—high-pitched squeaks and chirps.

• Prolonged exposure to water temperatures below 63–65° Fahrenheit (about 17–18° Celsius) can cause stress to manatees. They live mostly in warm climates.

• A manatee breathes through its nose; special flaps close when it dives. The lungs are located dorsally, or on the side of the body, and extend almost the length of the body cavity. They assist in keeping the manatee buoyant. Manatees may stay submerged for at least twenty minutes when resting, but when they are using a great deal of energy, they may surface to breathe every thirty seconds.

• The reproductive rate of a manatee is very slow; on average only one calf is born every two to three years in the Florida species and even longer in the Amazon species, perhaps every three to four years. A calf averages 3 to 4 feet (1 meter) in length at birth and can weigh 60 pounds (about 27 kilograms). The mother nurses the calf for approximately one year.

This Florida manatee has algae on his lip.

head

back

eye

nostrils

peduncle

whiskers

flippers with toenails

tail or fluke

65

Manatee Origins

Manatees belong to a mammal group called Paenungulata, sharing certain anatomical features with their distant relatives, the elephants. These features include nails on their flippers (like the nails on an elephant's foot) and large, muscular, flexible prehensile upper lips that act in many ways like shortened trunks. The earliest known fossil ancestor with hind limbs is Pezosiren, which was collected in Jamaica. Pezosiren, fifty million years ago, was a creature the size of a large pig that stood about three feet high. Although it could walk on land, it may well have spent most of its time in the water, like present-day hippos.

In ancient times there were as many as thirty-five species in the order Sirenia. Over time, the hind legs of Pezosiren disappeared and were replaced with a flat tail for swimming. The fossils, as the Sirenia evolved, show either weak hind limbs or vestigial—that is, unnecessary—external hind limbs. Modern manatees, of course, have only the front flippers—no hind limbs and no hind flippers.

Manatees as we know them today probably evolved from the Amazon region two million years ago and spread out from there into the Caribbean, all the way up to both coasts of Florida and to West Africa.

These Florida manatees are taking a rest on the ocean floor.

A mother and her calf; these are Florida manatees.

West Indian Manatee

Trichechus manatus

Fast fact: The West Indian manatee is the only species that is composed of two subspecies: the Florida manatee *Trichechus manatus latirostris*, which can be found year round in the coastal and river waters of the Florida peninsula; and the Antillean manatee *Trichechus manatus manatus*, which can be found anywhere from well south of the equator along the Brazilian coast, all the way north into Mexico, southern Texas, and such Caribbean Islands as Cuba, Hispaniola, Jamaica, and Puerto Rico. The Florida manatee is the best studied of all manatee species.

Appearance: Gray, sometimes more brownish.

Size: Approximately 10 feet (3 meters), but some measure 13 feet (4 meters). Generally 1,000 pounds (454 kilograms) but can exceed 3,000 pounds (1361 kilograms).

Speed: West Indian manatees swim in short bursts up to 20 mph (17 kph), but generally, like the other species, they move much more slowly, averaging 3–5 mph (3–4 kph).

Social structure: Florida manatees are social, but their social structure is loose, with animals merging to form transitory groups. The exception is mother-calf relationships, which last two years.

Population: It is estimated that there are approximately four thousand Florida manatees in the state of Florida.

Fast fact: Since manatees cannot tolerate water colder than 58° Fahrenheit (14° Celsius) for long periods of time, in winter Florida manatees move to natural and artificial sources of warm water provided by springs and power plants. In summer, manatees travel to feeding sites throughout Florida's rivers and coastal bays, and to shallow areas of the Gulf of Mexico.

Threats: The largest human-related, recognized threats to the Florida manatee population are loss of warm-water refuges, collisions with watercraft, being crushed or drowned in canal locks or floodgates, and ingestion of fishhooks and monofilament fishing line. Cold weather and red tides also kill and debilitate manatees, occasionally in very large numbers.

A Florida manatee (*Trichechus manatus latirostris*) floats in Crystal River.

This Florida manatee is suckling at its mother's breast.

Amazonian Manatee

Trichechus inunguis

Fast fact: The Amazonian manatee is the only manatee species that lives entirely in freshwater habitats. It can be found throughout the Amazon River and its tributaries in Brazil, Peru, Colombia, and Ecuador.

Appearance: Easy to distinguish owing to its smooth, rubbery skin, long pectoral flippers, and lack of nails at the end of flippers (the species name *inunguis* is Latin for "no nails"). They often have white or pink belly patches.

Size: These are the smallest of the manatees, rarely exceeding 9.2 feet (2.8 meters) in length. A large individual weighs 1,058 pounds (450 kilograms).

Population: Given their remote habitat, Amazonian manatees are not as well studied as manatees in Florida. Scientists have no real idea how many exist.

Fast fact: More than other manatee species, the Amazonian manatee is affected by the dry season. Scientists estimate that these manatees may fast during the dry seasons for as many as two hundred days. In remote areas of the Amazon during the dry season, when the animals congregate in one place, they are often hunted for food, even though they are protected by law.

Threats: The biggest threat for this species stems from assaults on the ecosystem. Deforestation in Latin America continues at a breakneck pace. Mining, oil drilling, lumber industries, and hunting continue to put great pressure on the Amazonian manatee.

The Naturama Foundation works with former manatee hunters to protect the species. Here a man returns a manatee calf to its mother in an Amazonian lake. The calf was captured by someone who tried to sell it, but the mother remained in the lake for several days, looking for her calf.

African Manatee

Trichechus senegalensis

Fast fact: The African manatee is the least studied of all the manatee species. Most biological and life history attributes are inferred from studies of the West Indian manatee.

Appearance: Similar to the West Indian manatee, but with a blunter snout, more protuberant eyes, and a body that is a bit more slender. They tend to have a more tubular shape than Florida manatees.

Size: Generally somewhat smaller than the West Indian manatee. Unfortunately, there are so few records of length and girth measurements for this species that details about the African manatee are unknown.

Social structure: Like Florida manatees, they are mostly solitary but can form groups for feeding or mating. Groups of more than ten individuals have been documented. Calves have a long period of dependency and probably stay with their mother for a year or more.

Fast fact: African manatees have been documented traveling in inshore ocean waters off Senegal, Guinea Bissau, Ivory Coast, Ghana, Nigeria, and Cameroon. However, they generally live in rivers, estuaries, and lagoons because this is where their food plants are and they also need to drink fresh water to survive.

Population: The total number of African manatees is unknown because of the difficulty in accessing manatee locations and the elusive nature of the species. The welfare of African manatees remains uncertain owing to lack of knowledge, hunting pressure, political instability, and coastal development.

Threats: In many African countries, the hunting of manatees for food consumption is common. In other countries the oil and other parts of the animal are used for medicinal purposes. In parts of some countries such as Nigeria, Gabon, and Cameroon, certain tribes revere the manatee. Tribal legends, customs, and superstitions protect it, and it is viewed as a water deity called Mamiwata. Mamiwata myths in various forms exist in every country where the African manatee appears, but the myths themselves vary in each location. While in some regions the mythical status of the manatee protects them, in others Mamiwata is something to be hunted because she lures men away from their families into her watery lair. The Ivory Coast, Senegal, and Cameroon have created specially protected manatee reserves and sanctuaries.

In some African countries, hunters build shrines using manatee bones, and then make offerings to ensure good hunting. This shrine includes manatee skulls, rib bones, a harpoon, and voodoo dolls.

Resources

Books of Interest

Hotta, Akemi. *Manatee*. Chronicle Books, 1998.

Powell, James. *Manatees: Natural History & Conservation*. WorldLife Library, Voyageur Press, 2002.

Reep, Roger L., and Robert K. Bonde. *The Florida Manatee: Biology and Conservation*, 1st edition. University Press of Florida, 2006.

Reynolds, John E., and Karen Glasser. *Mysterious Manatees*. University Press of Florida, 2003.

Reynolds, John E., and Daniel K. Odell. *Manatees and Dugongs*. Facts On File, 1991.

Ripple, Jeff. *Manatees and Dugongs of the World*. WorldLife Discovery Guides, Voyageur Press, 1999.

Sweeney, Gregory, and Karen Keberle. *Manatees: The Gentle Giants*. Cuttlefish Publishing, 2005.

Swinburne, Steve. *Saving Manatees*. Boyds Mills Press, 2009.

Websites of Interest

Serenian International
www.sirenian.org

The mission of Sirenian International is to ensure the long-term conservation of manatee and dugong populations and our shared aquatic habitats around the world through research, educational outreach, and capacity building.

Save the Manatee Club
www.savethemanatee.org

The mission of Save the Manatee Club is to protect endangered manatees and their aquatic habitats for future generations.

Save the Manatee Club's Position on Manatee Harassment and Swimming with Manatees: www.savethemanatee.org/ta_swimming_position_8-09.html

National Geographic Page on Manatees animals.nationalgeographic.com/animals/mammals/manatee.html

Florida Fish and Wildlife Conservation Commission (Florida Manatee Program)

A close-up of a Florida manatee's whiskers.

www.myfwc.com/WILD
LIFEHABITATS/Manatee_index.htm

*For responsible manatee swimming in
Crystal River, Florida*
www.fun2dive.com

*For more information on Mote Marine
Laboratory's Manatee Research Program*
www.mote.org
The primary goal of the Mote Marine
Laboratory Manatee Research Program
is to serve as an integral part of a team
devoted to studying manatees in Florida
and to provide scientific information of
value to managers and legislators who
seek to balance effective conservation
with human activities. The program's
vision is to remain one of the world's
leading centers for quality research
involving sirenians (manatees and dugongs), while developing approaches that
will affect research and conservation
efforts for marine mammals around
the globe.

Hugh and Buffett
isurus.mote.org/~hughbuffett/pages/
Kidz/kidz1.anat.phtml
Two favorite research manatees at Mote
Marine Laboratory in Sarasota, Florida.

*Lucy Keith Diagne's blog "In Search of
'Mamiwata'"*
insearchofmamiwata.blogspot.com
Mamiwata is an African name for a spirit
believed to be embodied by the manatee. This blog chronicles Lucy's search
for the elusive African manatee and her
exploration to understand its biology,
habitat and preservation needs, and
economic and cultural significance. So
little is known about this animal, yet it
is intensely hunted almost everywhere
it exists and may already be gone from
much of its previous range. In
2006 Lucy was inspired to try to
find African manatees and learn
more about them, starting in
Gabon.

IUCN Red List
www.iucnredlist.org/about/
red-list-overview
The IUCN Red List of Threatened Species is widely recognized as the most comprehen-
sive, objective global approach
for evaluating the conservation
status of plant and animal species.

IUCN's Red List of Threatened Species Page for Amazonian Manatee:
www.iucnredlist.org/apps/redlist/
details/22102/0

IUCN's Red List of Threatened Species
Page for West Indian Manatee:
www.iucnredlist.org/apps/redlist/
details/22106/0

IUCN's Red List of Threatened Species
Page for African Manatee:
www.iucnredlist.org/apps/redlist/
details/22104/0

This is an underside view of a Florida manatee rolling on its side.
You can see the nails on both flippers.

Author's Note

Swimming with manatees can be a lot of fun, but when thousands of people a day get into the water with these fascinating creatures, one has to wonder what the effect on the animals could be. Manatees are protected federally under the Marine Mammal Protection Act and the Endangered Species Act and at the state level under the Florida Manatee Sanctuary Act. Harassment of manatees is unlawful, yet manatee harassment in Florida is on the rise. I met some scientists who think that swimming with manatees, but not harassing or touching them, is a good thing because it gives people new respect and knowledge about the animal. This familiarity with manatees, they say, will help us put pressure on policymakers and managers to continue to conserve them. Others worry that perhaps too many people swimming with manatees might actually put a strain on their habitats and on the animals themselves. What do you think?

On another topic, scientists who collect data that will be used for the conservation of animals aren't always floating down rivers in dugout canoes or flying over power plants in small planes. They also spend much of their time in labs or in their offices, collecting and interpreting data from other scientists. In order for conservation managers to set policy to protect animals, they must draw information from a wide array of places and people—chemists, anthropologists, marine biologists, ecologists, and many other specialists. Protecting manatees is definitely a team effort.

As for the relationship between science and conservation, Dr. John Reynolds, who has experience in the field, in the lab, and in the United States Congress, emphasizes that the practice of science is not the same thing as the practice of conservation. "Data and science," he says, "can lead to improved conservation, but only if that science is communicated properly." Conservation, he says, is the hard part. "Science is pretty straightforward. You develop a question or hypothesis and you develop a method of testing it. But blending a variety of human values and policies and regulations with that science to come up with an outcome that allows species and people to persist—that's tough."

I encourage everyone to make conservation of species a priority in our pursuit of science as we come to know more about manatees and other species.

The author, Peter Lourie, poses with a manatee sign in Manaus, Brazil. The sign reads PRESERVE THE AMAZONIAN MANATEE!

Glossary

aerial survey: data collected by scientists from airplanes

baseline health information: information gathered at the beginning of a study to determine the overall health of a population, from which variations in future studies can be measured.

biomarker: a biological or chemical response to a stimulus or stressor. For example, if a manatee moves out of the way of a boat, that's a biomarker. The field of biomarkers generally involves measurable biochemical changes from a particular environmental or human-related factor, including but not limited to stressors such as contaminants, disease, and nutritional deficiencies.

biomass: the total mass of organisms (plants and animals) in a given area.

conservation biology: a combined approach to the protection and management of species. Conservation biology draws on many fields and disciplines, from basic biological fields such as genetics and ecology to the social sciences of anthropology and sociology, as well as resource management fields such as fisheries.

conservation manager: a general term for a person who uses data from natural, scientific, sociological, anthropological, and economic studies to develop strategies that promote conservation of species or habitat.

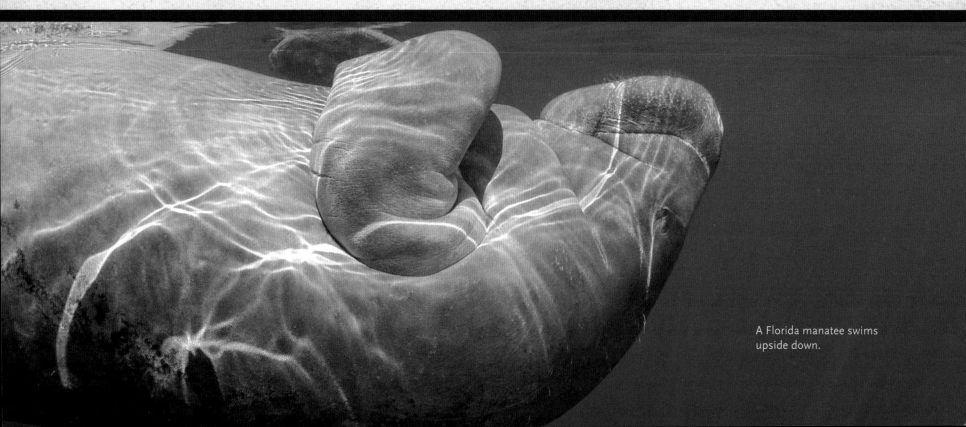

A Florida manatee swims upside down.

conservation status: a measure of how likely a species is to exist in the near term (years) or longer term (decades). Many factors are used to assess a species' conservation status, including the number of individuals remaining, the assumed percent of the population that is mature, the presumed overall increase or decrease in the population over time, survival (or the opposite, mortality) rates, and the extent to which threats to the species or its habitat are identified and mitigated.

contaminant: a chemical impurity such as pesticides and man-made oil that may poison manatees and affect their ability to reproduce.

dugong: a mammal similar in shape and size to the manatee that falls into the order Sirenia and lives in the Indo-Pacific region. Unlike the manatee, the dugong has a forked fluke, smooth skin, and no nails on its flippers. The Stellar's sea cow, an extinct species of toothless dugong, was twice the size of a manatee (up to thirty feet or nine meters).

endangered species: a group of genetically related organisms (that is, a species) that are at risk of becoming extinct because they either are few in number or are at risk from environmen-tal, human, or natural dangers.

extinct: in biology, when the last individual of a species no longer exists, having died out leaving no existing representatives.

gene: the unit of heredity in chromosomes; a segment of double-stranded DNA.

genetics: the study of genes and heredity, or how characteristics are passed from parents to children.

girth measurements: the circumference of standard anatomical sites around the body, usually done with a tape measure.

herbivore: an animal whose diet is composed primarily of plant matter.

igapó: a type of Amazonian flooded forest that occurs along rivers. This type of forest has lower-nutrient soil, lower biomass, and less diversity than other flooded forests in the same region.

mammal: a warm-blooded vertebrate characterized by its having had hair or fur at some point in its life, the secretion of milk by females for the nourishment of the young, and (typically) the birth of live young (as opposed to the laying of eggs).

peduncle: the base of the manatee fluke, where it connects to the body.

physiology: the study of how living organisms and their body systems function.

radio transmitter: an electronic device that emits a radio signal, usually with the aid of an antenna.

satellite tracking: an important part of conservation research that involves determining animal movements and habitat use. Satellite tracking also gives biologists the ability to locate the study animal in order to observe its behavior.

sirenian: a mammal in the scientific order Sirenia, which includes manatees and dugongs. These animals are herbivores and have two forelimbs and a flattened fluke, or tail, and spend most of their lives in water.

subsistence: means by which one maintains life; a means of surviving.

telemetry: technology that allows the study of an animal from a distance. Examples include devices such as satellite tags that can give the GPS position of an animal as well as record the number of times it dives (and the water temperature) in a given time period.

Photo Credits

Capt. Joseph Detrick/
www.fun2dive.com: 3, 4, (both
images), 6 (both), 9, 24 (both), 26 (inset),
27 (bottom), 33 (bottom), 64, 65, 66, 67,
68, 69, 73, 75, 80

Humberto Bahena/ECOSUR: 8, 27
(top), 28, 29 (center and top), 35 (center),
36, 38

Anselmo d'Affonseca/LMA/
INPA: 11

Hercules Quelu: 16 (center)

John Reynolds and Florida
Power & Light Company: 25

Lucy Keith Diagne: 29 (right), 40, 42
(right), 43, 44 (left), 45 (center), 46, 47,
48 (both), 49 (all), 50 (top left, bottom),
51, 52, 53 (right), 54, 56, 57 (both)

U.S. Geological Survey, Sirenia
Project: 35 (inset), 37 (both images)

Tomas Diagne: 41, 42 (left), 53 (left),
55 (both images)

Gabriel Segniag-
beto: 50 (top right), 71

Fundación
Natûtama: 70

All other photos
by Peter Lourie

Author and photographer Peter Lourie in the field.

Index

A Florida manatee reaches neutral buoyancy. This means the manatee will neither sink nor rise.